A·C·T·I·O·N B·O

DISCOVER THE
TITANIC

Eric Kentley

DORLING KINDERSLEY

LONDON • • SYDNEY

A DORLING KINDERSLEY BOOK

Project Editor Claire Bampton
Senior Editor Sue Leonard
Art Editors Jane Bull, Cathy Chesson
Picture Researcher Tom Worsley
Photographer Steve Gorton
Paper Engineer David Hawcock

Illustrator Hans Jenssen

Managing Editor Sarah Phillips
Senior Managing Art Editor Peter Bailey
DTP Designers Karen Nettelfield, Andrew O'Brien
Design Assistant Miranda May
Production Joanne Blackmore, Lauren Britton

First published in Great Britain in 1997
by Dorling Kindersley Limited
9 Henrietta Street, London WC2E 8PS

2 4 6 8 10 9 7 5 3

Copyright © 1997 Dorling Kindersley Limited, London

Visit us on the World Wide Web at http://www.dk.com

A CIP catalogue record for this book is available
from the British Library.

ISBN: 0-7513-5624-7

Colour reproduction by Flying Colours, Italy
Manufactured in China for Imago

Security clearance

This is your identity card. Access to the site of the wreck is strictly
controlled, so please fill in your details and attach a photograph of
yourself in the space provided.
Present it to the security staff
at Ponta Delgada quayside.
They will allow you to board
the research vessel *Nadir*, and
join the expedition to the
wreck of the *Titanic*.

During the
expedition you
should display your
badge at all times.

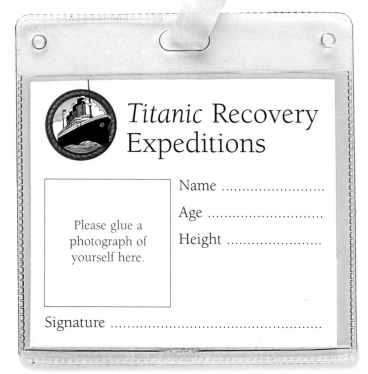

Titanic Recovery Expeditions

Please glue a
photograph of
yourself here.

Name ....

Age ....

Height ....

Signature ....

Explorer's tasks

Your expedition is divided into three stages: the trip out to the
site of the wreck on the *Nadir*, a tour around the *Titanic* in
Nautile, and raising and restoring objects from the wreck for
display in an exhibition. For each stage you will have an
expedition leader who will set you a number of explorer's tasks.
Work through the tasks carefully on a separate piece of paper.
You can then check whether your answers are correct on page 30.

The *Nadir*
and *Nautile*

Titanic Recovery Expeditions

Congratulations! You have been successful in your application to visit the wreck of the most famous ship in the world, the *Titanic*. Your expedition will start at the quayside at Ponta Delgada, in the Azores. There you will set sail, on the *Nadir*, and travel to the spot where the *Titanic* sank more than 85 years ago. You will then descend in a submersible (small submarine) called *Nautile* to the seabed where the wreck lies. After a tour of the *Titanic*, you will recover some objects from the site of the wreck. Back on board the *Nadir*, you will learn how to restore them for display in an exhibition aimed at keeping the legend of the *Titanic* alive. Three experienced expedition leaders will tell you about the *Titanic* and help you during your voyage.

Enjoy yourself – and "bon voyage"!

ITINERARY

Claes Zachary –
Master of the *Nadir*

George D'Addario –
Pilot of *Nautile*

Diana Barton –
Conservator

STAGE 1
During the first stage of your journey you will sail across the Atlantic to the site of the wreck of the *Titanic*.

STAGE 2
During the second stage of your journey you will descend to the seabed and embark on a tour of the wreck. You will visit different parts of the ship and piece together the events that took place just before and immediately after the *Titanic* sank.

STAGE 3
During the third stage of your journey you will raise objects from the seabed and set them up for display in an exhibition.

Crossing the Atlantic

"Hello and welcome on board. I'm Claes Zachary, the master of the research vessel *Nadir*. I'm going to tell you where we're going, and how we will get there."

■ The *Titanic's* doomed voyage began at Southampton, England, on Wednesday 10 April 1912. After stopping at Cherbourg, France, and Queenstown in Ireland, the *Titanic* set out across the Atlantic Ocean the following day, planning to reach New York seven days later. She sank in the early hours of 15 April. Sailing in the *Nadir* it will take us four and a half days to reach the spot where the *Titanic* sank.

THE FATEFUL VOYAGE

When the *Titanic* was completed in 1912, she was the largest and, for the first-class passengers, the most luxurious ship in the world. Thought to be unsinkable, the *Titanic* sank on her maiden (first) voyage. Hundreds died, including some of the world's richest people.

The *Nadir* and *Nautile*
The *Nadir* is the vessel that will carry the submersible *Nautile* to the site of the wreck. She has a crew of 15, but she also carries 14 people to maintain and staff *Nautile*. This leaves space for ten other expedition members, including you.

Ocean liners
Before passenger planes were available, many shipping firms ran services across the Atlantic. The *Titanic*, owned by the White Star Line, carried passengers and mail and so was called the RMS (Royal Mail Steamer) *Titanic*.

R.M.S. TITANIC.

Stays held main mast in position

Main mast

Docking bridge

Rudder

Draught marks

Central propeller

Starboard propeller

Stay

An electric crane was used for loading stores and equipment.

STARBOARD (RIGHT-HAND) SIDE OF THE *TITANIC*

Funnels allowed smoke to escape from the boiler rooms.

Lifeboats

Radio aerial

Compass platform

Navigating across the Atlantic

In 1912, ships like the *Titanic* used a combination of speed, compass, clock, and astronomical observations to estimate their position. Modern ships record their position using degrees longitude, which measure how far east or west they are, and degrees latitude, which show how far north or south they are. At the North Pole (90° N) the North Star is almost directly overhead.

TASK 1

If a ship starts out from 30° W, 40° N, where is it leaving?

TASK 2

The ship sails along the same line of latitude until it reaches 76° W. Where is it?

TASK 3

The ship sails again, this time until it reaches 40° W and 20° S. Can its passengers see the North Star?

North Star

TIP
The farther south a ship sails, the lower the North Star appears in the sky. Once a ship sails south of the Equator, the star disappears completely.

Line of vision from Earth's surface to North Star

North Pole

Earth

Lines of latitude

ROUTES ACROSS THE ATLANTIC

The *Titanic* travelled faster than we will in the *Nadir*. She took less than three and a half days to travel from Queenstown to the point where she sank. The route the *Titanic* took was often used in the cold months to avoid the worst ice fields and icebergs.

LONGITUDE   60° W   40° W   20° W   0°

GREENLAND

CANADA

NORTH ATLANTIC OCEAN

60° N

NEWFOUNDLAND

Queenstown   IRELAND   UNITED KINGDOM   50° N

Route taken by the Titanic in 1912

FRANCE

Southampton

Cherbourg

Site of the wreck of the Titanic

Route we will take in the Nadir

SPAIN   40° N

AZORES

LATITUDE

TITANIC MYSTERY

Before the *Titanic* sank, her officers calculated her position to be more than 13 miles away from where the wreck was eventually discovered. This may be one of the reasons why it took more than 70 years to find her.

Destination the *Titanic*

The wreck is about 560 km (350 miles) off the Newfoundland coast, and more than 1,600 km (1,000 miles) from New York. When we leave the Azores behind, you will not see any land until we return.

The navigation satellites are always in the same position above Earth.

The *Nadir* receives signals from the satellites to plot her position accurately.

Navigating the *Nadir*

The *Nadir* uses satellites to navigate. When it is above the wreck, a sonar records the shape of the seabed and locates the wreck's precise position.

Surface of ocean

The *Nadir*

Seabed

The pulses of sound are echoed back to the *Nadir* and are used to make up a picture of the seabed.

A sonar on board the *Nadir* sends pulses of sound to the seabed.

The water line indicated how deep the *Titanic* should sit in the water.

Navigation room

The wheelhouse contained steering equipment.

Foremast

Stay

Crow's-nest

Shrouds

Anchor crane

Bridge

Starboard anchor

Draught marks measured how deep the *Titanic* sat in the water.

Search and Discovery

■ We are now directly above where the wreck of the *Titanic* lies on the seabed. Immediately after the disaster, people talked about recovering the *Titanic*, but even if she had been located, the technology to reach her was not available. The tools necessary for deep-sea exploration were developed only in the late 1970s. It was then that the search for the *Titanic* began in earnest.

The Atlantic Ocean
The natural features of the mid-Atlantic seabed are a complicated mixture of hills, plains, and valleys. The greatest depth is 8,742 m (28,681 ft).

The *Titanic* was found at a depth of 3,798 m (12,460 ft) at the base of a continental shelf.

EXPLORING THE SEABED

In 1985 Dr. Robert Ballard led a successful American/French expedition to find the *Titanic*. In two months the research ships *Le Suroit* and the *Knorr* surveyed over 260 square km (100 square miles) of Atlantic seabed using sonar and an unmanned submersible called *Argo*.

A continental shelf is a shallow area next to land.

Base of continental shelf

Site of the sunken wreck of the *Titanic*

Underwater navigation

Signals from satellites, used for navigation on the surface, cannot be picked up underwater. Submersibles like *Argo* use underwater transponders that fix their position with the main ship. A submersible can then send out and receive signals from the transponders to plot its position.

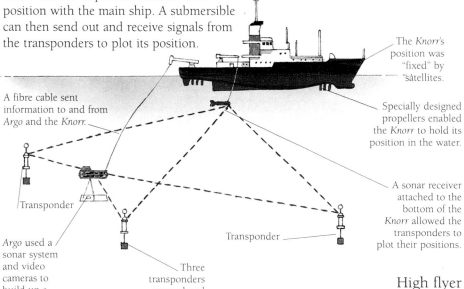

A fibre cable sent information to and from *Argo* and the *Knorr*.

The *Knorr's* position was "fixed" by satellites.

Specially designed propellers enabled the *Knorr* to hold its position in the water.

Transponder

Argo used a sonar system and video cameras to build up a picture of the seabed.

Three transponders were placed underwater to enable *Argo* to plot her precise position.

Transponder

A sonar receiver attached to the bottom of the *Knorr* allowed the transponders to plot their positions.

THE *KNORR*/*ARGO* TRANSPONDER NET

High flyer

Here *Argo* is being launched from the *Knorr*. *Argo* is a remote-controlled deep-towed deep-sea video vehicle. This unmanned submersible was connected to the *Knorr* by a very long fibre cable.

FLYING *ARGO* TO FIND THE *TITANIC*

Remote control
A pilot "flew" *Argo* with a joystick from the safety of the *Knorr*'s control room.

Filming the seabed
Argo's video cameras sent forward, down, and enlarged views of the seabed to the *Knorr*.

The *Titanic* found
At 1 a.m., on 1 September 1985 *Argo*'s pilot saw this image on the video monitor. It is the front of one of the *Titanic*'s boilers. Ballard's team had found the wreck!

The real thing
It was one of these boilers that was spotted by *Argo*'s video cameras.

The *Atlantis II* carried *Alvin* out to the site of the sinking.

Touring the *Titanic*
On 13 July 1986, Ballard returned to the site of the wreck to make the first manned dive to the sunken *Titanic*. He did this in a submersible called *Alvin*.

Alvin was launched from the stern of the *Atlantis II*.

☆
TITANIC MYSTERY

Ballard's team spotted the first sign of the *Titanic* wreckage at 1 a.m. on 1 September 1985. The British newspaper *The Observer* announced the story the same day. Because of the different time zones this means the story must have been printed at least eight hours before the discovery was made! Did someone know where the *Titanic* was all the time?

The robotic eye
Alvin can take three people to the seabed. It can also carry *Jason Junior*, a remote-controlled robot that can explore inside the wreck. The small robot is piloted from inside *Alvin*. It carries its own lights, still camera, and video camera to record the wreck.

★ EXPLORER'S TASK ⓑ

Finding the *Titanic*
To help locate the *Titanic*, Ballard used both an echo-sounder and a sonar. He used an echo-sounder to measure the depth of the sea, and a sonar to build up pictures of the seabed. An echo-sounder beams a pulse of sound down to the seabed, where it is reflected just like an echo. Sonars work in the same way, but send out fan-shaped beams of sound.

TASK 1
In diagram **a**, if the echo is picked up six seconds after being sent, how deep is the water? a) 6,000 m (19,684 ft) b) 3,000 m (9,842 ft) c) 60,000 m (196,848 ft)

TASK 2
In diagram **b**, would all the echoes from the seabed arrive at the same time? Why?

Echo-sounder

a

TIP
Sound travels through water at about 1,000 mps (3,280 fps).

Echoes of sound

Seabed

Sonar

b

TIP
Think about how a picture of the seabed is built up.

Seabed

Echoes of sound

The Yellow Submarine

"Hello, I'm George D'Addario, pilot of *Nautile*. As we dive, I'll tell you how *Nautile* works. Then, when we reach the seabed, I'll guide you around the most famous wreck in the world."

■ Once we have boarded *Nautile*, she is taken to the stern (back end) of the *Nadir*, where a specially designed crane will swing her out and release her into the water. *Nautile* then drops down 3,798 m (12,460 ft) to the seabed. Our descent takes an hour and a half, but after the first few minutes it will be too dark to see anything. Go to the toilet before we leave – you will not get another chance for 11 hours!

Dropping off

As *Nautile* descends you will hardly notice any movement. During the dive, *Nautile* navigates by receiving signals from the *Nadir* and from transponders in the water around the wreck. She sends pictures to the *Nadir* through her own transmitter.

Keeping watch

Nautile carries three people: the pilot, the co-pilot, and yourself. When you reach the seabed keep a careful watch through your porthole – there is always the danger of hitting the wreck.

NAUTILE

Submersibles like *Nautile* are small submarines that can only work underwater for a few hours. *Nautile* has a top speed of 1.7 knots (3 kph/2 mph). Her thrusters and hinged propeller make her highly manoeuvrable.

Sonar builds up a picture of the seabed.

Hook-up used by the *Nadir*'s crane to hoist *Nautile* back on deck

Lateral thruster

Spotlights illuminate the wreck.

Video cameras record the wreck.

The co-pilot's porthole

The co-pilot navigates and controls the cameras.

Portholes for the pilot and yourself

Two robotic arms pick up objects from the seabed.

Robin is secured to *Nautile* during the descent.

Sink or swim

Before you descend, *Nautile's* technicians will ask you your weight. This is because they must fill the ballast bags to the right weight so that *Nautile* will sink to the seabed. The bags are filled with steel shot and will be left on the seabed.

SCALE ILLUSTRATION SHOWING THE
NADIR IN RELATION TO THE *TITANIC*

Surface of water

Deepest scuba dive is 133 m (437 ft)

500 m (1,640 ft)

Operating depth for naval submarines is 762 m (2,500 ft).

1,000 m (3,280 ft)

Powerful spotlight

Video cameras

Portholes

Lights, cameras, action

The wreck of the *Titanic* is so deep that natural light could never reach it. So *Nautile* must take powerful spotlights with her. *Nautile* also carries one fixed and one movable video camera, which run constantly once she reaches the seabed.

Diving deep

Nautile is one of the few vessels in the world that can dive as deep as the *Titanic* wreck. In fact she can dive almost half as far again, to 6,000 m (19,684 ft) and reach 97 per cent of the world's ocean beds.

2,000 m (6,561 ft)

Robin

To film inside the wreck, *Nautile* can carry *Robin*, a tethered and remote-controlled video camera. It is operated from within *Nautile*.

3,000 m (9,842 ft)

Acoustic head used for navigation

VHF antenna picks up acoustic signals from the *Nadir*

Wreck of the *Titanic* is at 3,798 m (12,460 ft)

Nautile can dive to 6,000 m (19,684 ft)

4,000 m (13,123 ft)

Lateral thruster

Nautile carries enough oxygen to last five days underwater in case of an emergency.

Hinged propeller

Echo-sounder charts depth of water

Main batteries power *Nautile* for 12 hours

EXPLORER'S TASK C

Navigating underwater

Transponders are placed, using satellite navigation, around the wreck of the *Titanic*. Sound signals from *Nautile* are picked up by the transponders, which immediately send back a sound signal. By working out how far away each transponder is, *Nautile's* computers calculate her position.

TASK 1

Nautile receives a signal from transponder **a** after two seconds, transponder **b** one second later, and transponder **c** after another second. Work out how far away transponders **a**, **b**, and **c** are from *Nautile* so that the computer can plot your position.

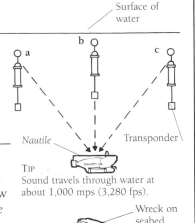

Surface of water

a   b   c

Nautile   Transponder

TIP
Sound travels through water at about 1,000 mps (3,280 fps).

Wreck on seabed

The Wreck of the *Titanic*

■ *Nautile* will land on the seabed some distance from the wreck to avoid any possibility of damage. We will switch on her spotlights and travel over the bottom until you get your first view of the *Titanic* – of her bow, which ploughed into the the seabed. The range of the spotlights is not very great, so your view will be limited. Lie down flat, look out of your porthole, and get ready to begin the tour.

BELFAST GIANT

The *Titanic* and her sister ship, the *Olympic,* were built in Belfast in Ireland, at the Harland and Wolff shipyard. The *Titanic's* first keel plate was laid on 31 March 1909. On 31 May 1911 she was launched, but as an empty shell. The interior was then completed and she was finally ready for sea trials by the end of March 1912. More than 11,300 workers helped build the *Titanic*.

Your first glimpse

If you look ahead, you will see the huge bow of the *Titanic* towering over us. As we rise you will notice that rivers of "rust" cascade down her sides, covering her name.

Building the *Titanic*

Three hundred and fifty steel frames, with ten levels of deck supports, formed the skeleton of the *Titanic*. Steel plates, up to 1.8 m (6 ft) high, 11 m (36 ft) wide, and weighing 4.5 tonnes (4.4 tons) were riveted to the frames.

Touring the wreck

When the *Titanic* sank, she split in half. This model shows the bow section of the wreck. We will be exploring both halves during our tour.

The *Titanic*

Nautile   The *Nadir*

Comparing sizes

This diagram shows the size of the *Titanic* in comparison to the *Nadir* and *Nautile*. The *Titanic* was 269 m (883 ft) long, *Nadir* is 56 m (184 ft) long, and *Nautile* is just 8 m (26 ft) long. The *Titanic* was 34 times longer than *Nautile*.

The *Titanic* broke into two sections between her third and fourth funnels.

How ships float

If you drop a solid piece of steel into water, it sinks. So how can a huge ship float? The answer is that because a ship's hull is hollow, the weight of water it displaces is more than the weight of ship and cargo. The weight of this displaced water leads to an upthrust, or force, which makes the ship seem lighter in the water.

TASK 1

The *Titanic* weighed 46,000 tonnes (45,273 tons) and displaced 60,000 tonnes (59,052 tons) of water. The *Nadir* weighs 980 tonnes (965 tons) and displaces 2,025 tonnes (1,993 tons) of water. Look at diagrams **a** and **b**, which give two options for the *Titanic*, and **c**, which relates to the *Nadir*, and work out whether, once crew, passengers, and cargo have been added, the ships would float or sink.

The *Titanic* **a**

Crew, passengers, and cargo weigh 20,000 tonnes (19,684 tons)

The *Titanic* **b**

Crew, passengers, and cargo weigh 10,000 tonnes (9,842 tons)

The *Nadir* **c**

Crew, passengers, and cargo weigh 1,000 tonnes (984 tons)

Anchoring the ship

All of the *Titanic's* bow anchors are still in place. Such a large vessel needed three anchors to moor it. The 15.75-tonne (15.5-ton) centre anchor lies here, useless, on the forecastle deck.

Spick and span

This is how the anchor looked in 1912. The chains were attached to the port (left-hand) and starboard (right-hand) anchors.

The debris field is approximately 2.6 km (1 mile) square.

TITANIC MYSTERY

Analysis of the steel of the *Titanic* has revealed a high sulphur content. In cold water, such as that found in the mid-Atlantic on the night of 14 April 1912, this could have made the *Titanic's* steel hull plates brittle. Could the quality of the steel have contributed to the sinking of the ship?

Gymnasium roof

Davit for lowering lifeboats

Remains of the foremast

Stern of wreck

Coal from the *Titanic's* boiler rooms

Debris field

Bow of wreck

MAP SHOWING THE SITE OF THE *TITANIC'S* WRECK

Our tour plan

During our tour we will be visiting various parts of the wreck of the *Titanic*. We will tour the public areas (A), the engines and boiler rooms (B), the crow's nest and the bow (C), the bridge (D), the upper deck (E), and the debris field (F).

Bunker hatch for coal

Anchor crane

Anchor

The Floating Palace

■ As we move around the wreck in *Nautile*, look carefully for the signs that show how magnificent the *Titanic* was in 1912. Deep within the ship lie the remains of spacious dining rooms, luxurious staterooms, elegant cafés, libraries, Turkish baths, a swimming pool, a gymnasium, and even a barbershop. On the *Titanic*, the accommodation for some passengers was more comfortable than their own homes!

ALL ABOARD

During the voyage, the *Titanic* was kept in good running order by an extensive crew. Captain Smith was in command of the 891 crew members. He had been a White Star captain for 25 years. This was to be his final voyage before retiring.

Captain Smith

Manning the ship

The ship's crew were divided into three departments: the Deck Department of 73 people, including officers and seamen; the Engine Department of 325; and the Steward's Department of 494.

A la carte restaurant

Verandah and Palm Court Café

Second-class library

Café Parisien
First-class smoking room

Aft first-class staircase

First-class suite rooms

First-class staterooms

First-class dining saloon

Second-class dining room

Second-class cabins

First-class suite rooms

Hospital

First-class staterooms

Saloon bar

First-class staterooms

This deck bench is from one of the ship's promenades.

Seating at the stern

All three classes were kept separate. This promenade was where the third-class passengers could sit and relax or go for a stroll.

This gold-plated light fixture still hangs in place in the entrance hall.

Reading lights

Electric lights illuminated the first-class reading and writing room. This room was mainly used by women, unlike the smoking room, which was reserved for men.

The grand staircase

Skylight

Clock

Passenger accommodation

The accommodation in the *Titanic* was arranged in rooms that contained varying numbers of berths (beds). The table below shows you how many rooms there were, and how many berths each room could hold.

PASSENGER ACCOMMODATION							
Number of rooms							
	1-berth	2-berth	3-berth	4-berth	6-berth	8-berth	10-berth
First class	96	106	127	-	-	-	-
Second class	-	76	2	129	-	-	-
Third class	-	66	-	112	37	5	2

NOTE: If required, 46 of the first-class 1-berth rooms could be converted into 2-berth rooms. Also, an extra 164 third-class passengers could sleep in open berths (dormitories).

TASK 1

Using the table and the note, work out the maximum number of passengers the *Titanic* could accommodate.

The grand staircase

The main forward staircase was one of the most dramatic features of the *Titanic*. It was lit by natural light through a huge domed skylight.

☆
TITANIC MYSTERY

Almost 50 passengers cancelled their place on the *Titanic* before it sailed. One of the cancellers was J.P. Morgan, owner of International Mercantile Marine (the owners of the White Star Line). Why did so many people cancel their trip?

Reading and writing room

First-class lounge

Private promenade

Gymnasium

Grand staircase

First-class staterooms

First-class suite rooms

Third-class cabins

Third-class dining saloon

Sauna and steam room

Turkish baths

First-class reception room

Swimming pool

First-class staterooms

Third-class cabins

This leaded window is from the first-class dining saloon.

The Captain's table

Captain Smith would dine with passengers at a table for six in the first-class dining saloon. The dining saloon could seat more than 500 people.

These windows look into one of the first-class rooms.

Travelling in style

The first-class rooms were large and luxurious. A first-class passenger paid about ten times as much as a third-class passenger.

Propeller Power

■ We will now leave the bow section of the *Titanic* and make the 2.4-km (1.5-mile) journey to the stern section. Here you will see the heart of the ship – the machinery that pushed her through the water. The *Titanic* was a triple-screw steamer. This means that she had three screws, or propellers, all powered by steam. Once you see one of the propellers you will begin to realize what an enormous ship the *Titanic* was.

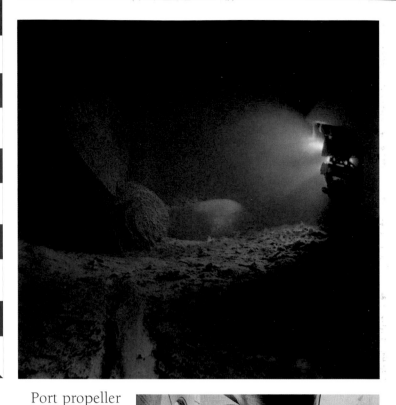

POWERING THE *TITANIC*

The *Titanic* had two types of engine: a turbine engine and four reciprocating engines. Steam was produced in the six boiler rooms and piped to the engine rooms. The reciprocating engines turned the port and starboard propellers and the turbine powered the central propeller. Once it had passed through the engines, the steam was piped to the condensers where it cooled back into water, which could be used again.

CUTAWAY OF THE *TITANIC* SHOWING ENGINES AND BOILER ROOMS

Port propeller
This is the port propeller, which was knocked out of position when it crashed on the seabed.

The starboard propeller, like the port propeller, is 7 m (23.5 ft) in diameter.

The fourth funnel was used for ventilation.

The ship's funnels
Three of the funnels took smoke from the boilers, but the fourth funnel was a fake to make the ship look more impressive.

The central propeller had four blades and was 5 m (16.5 ft) in diameter.

The port and starboard propellers had three blades.

The turbine shaft was 52 cm (20.5 in) in diameter.

There were two main condensers in the turbine room.

The turbine engine was in an iron casing, and weighed about 420 tonnes (413 tons).

Turbine engine room

Reciprocating engine room

Engine cylinders

Boiler room 1 contained five single-ended boilers.

How much fuel?

The amount of energy generated by a fuel is called its higher heating value and is measured in joules. The lower heating value is the amount of energy the fuel *actually* produces and depends on the efficiency of the engine in which the fuel is being used, and how much energy is lost due to evaporation and impurities.

TASK 1

If the higher heating value of coal is 30,000 million joules per tonne (30,481 million joules per ton) and the lower heating value of the coal on board the *Titanic* was ten per cent of the higher heating value, work out approximately how much coal the *Titanic* needed at the start of the journey.

TIP
Before the *Titanic* set sail it was estimated that she needed to produce approximately 18,000,000 million joules of energy to reach New York. When you do your calculations remember that one million = 1,000,000.

Colossal cylinders
The *Titanic*'s reciprocating engines were the largest ever built – over 9 m (30 ft) high. Each engine had four cylinders through which steam passed.

Keeping it going
Seventy-three trimmers and 177 firemen worked in the boiler rooms. Trimmers broke up coal into small lumps for the firemen to load into the boiler furnaces.

Excess steam could be released from the safety valves on either side of the funnels.

The uptakes led to the funnels.

The circular doors on the boilers led to furnaces – there were a total of 159.

Boilers
The *Titanic* had 29 boilers, each over 5 m (16.5 ft) high. All 24 double-ended boilers are still within the bow section. The five single-ended ones are scattered around the debris field.

Boiler rooms 2 to 5 each contained five double-ended boilers.

Coal bunker

The boilers were housed in watertight compartments.

The steam was carried to the engine rooms via steel pipes.

Smoke and waste gases were fed away from boilers through the uptakes.

Boiler room 6 contained four double-ended boilers.

Disaster Strikes

■ Inside *Nautile* the temperature has dropped to 2° C (35.6° F), the same as the water outside, so you may be feeling the cold. However, on the night of 14 April 1912 the sea temperature was even colder – it was below freezing. There was no trace of a wind, the sea was calm, and although the moon was not visible, there were many stars. As we move around the wreck, I will tell you more about the night of the disaster.

Icy waters
During her voyage, the *Titanic* received many ice warnings from other ships in the North Atlantic and as a precaution she took a course some 26 km (16 miles) south of the normal route. However, she did not slow down. On the night of the disaster she was travelling quite fast – about 20.5 knots (38 kph/24 mph).

Ship's light

Foremast

Bell

Warning lamp
This is the remains of the ship's mast light. High up on the foremast, it showed other ships which way the *Titanic* was travelling.

The crow's-nest was 15 m (50 ft) above the deck.

The crow's-nest
On the fallen foremast you can just make out the crow's-nest. In 1912 the crow's-nest contained a bell and a telephone for contacting the ship's bridge, and two people kept a constant lookout for icebergs and other ships.

The lookouts reached the crow's-nest via a ladder inside the foremast.

Lookout's bell
At 11.40 p.m. on 14 April 1912, Lookout Frederick Fleet saw an iceberg. He rang this bell, picked up the phone, and said "Iceberg right ahead".

Officers on the bridge were steering the ship.

HITTING THE ICEBERG

The alert from the lookout came too late for the *Titanic* to avoid the iceberg and it scraped along the starboard side of the ship. Although most of the passengers and crew felt only a slight jar, underwater the iceberg was creating a 91-m (300-ft) split in the *Titanic's* hull.

☆

TITANIC MYSTERY

The *Titanic's* bow is now buried deep in the seabed, so no-one knows what the iceberg really did to the ship's hull. There are two main theories as to how the *Titanic* actually sank. At first people thought that the iceberg cut a long gash; more probably it buckled the hull plates – perhaps sheering off some of the rivets and forcing the plates apart. Either way water would have then flooded through the gap, causing the great ship to sink.

Ice in the Atlantic

Ice was not unusual at these latitudes in April. The *Titanic* had actually received six warnings from other ships, and the men in the crow's-nest had been specifically told to keep a sharp lookout for icebergs. But it was not working practice to slow down until ice was actually spotted.

Artist's impression of the *Titanic* hitting the iceberg

The ice field

This is an artist's impression of the ice field into which the *Titanic* was sailing. It was over 10 km (6 miles) wide.

The iceberg seemed to have a scar of paint along it.

Atlantic iceberg

The day after the disaster, this iceberg was spotted near where the *Titanic* sank. It was between 15 and 30 m (50 and 100 ft) high.

EXPLORER'S TASK

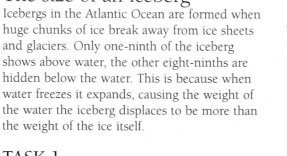

(G)

The size of an iceberg

Icebergs in the Atlantic Ocean are formed when huge chunks of ice break away from ice sheets and glaciers. Only one-ninth of the iceberg shows above water, the other eight-ninths are hidden below the water. This is because when water freezes it expands, causing the weight of the water the iceberg displaces to be more than the weight of the ice itself.

TASK 1

Using the diagram, work out the volume of ice below the water if the volume of ice seen above water is 12,500 cubic metres (441,375 cubic ft).

TASK 2

Now that you have calculated the volume of the ice below the water, work out the total volume of the iceberg.

Ice above water

Water level

Ice below water

TIP
Remember that only one-ninth of the iceberg is visible above the water.

"CQD – Sinking Fast!"

■ We are now moving around the area where the *Titanic's* bridge once stood. This was the control centre, where the captain and officers steered the ship, ordered the speed of its engines, and plotted its course. Imagine the scene on the bridge when the iceberg hit the ship, water started flooding in, and the captain and officers quickly had to decide on the best action to take.

ICE AHEAD

On hearing that there was an iceberg ahead, First Officer Murdoch ordered the engines to be stopped and put in reverse. He also ordered the wheel to be turned "Hard a' starboard". Although this steered the ship away from the iceberg, it was not quick enough to avoid a collision.

CUTAWAY OF THE *TITANIC* SHOWING THE FLOODING CAUSED BY THE ICEBERG

The ship's wireless (radio) was operated in the Marconi room by two employees of the Marconi Company.

The bridge contained telegraphs to communicate with the engine rooms.

First Officer Murdoch

Wheelhouse

The bridge

Captain Smith rushed to the bridge as soon as he felt the collision. Now the bridge is almost unrecognizable. Only the base of the wheelhouse, and the telemotor to which the steering wheel was attached, mark the spot.

The iceberg scraped along the starboard side of the ship.

At the time of the disaster there were five men on duty on the bridge.

☆
TITANIC MYSTERY

Murdoch's actions nearly saved the ship. If the iceberg had been spotted a few seconds earlier, the disaster could have been avoided. So why were the lookouts not given binoculars, even though the ship was carrying them?

The bulkhead between boiler rooms 5 and 6 gave way at about 12.45 a.m.

If the first four compartments had flooded, rather than the first five, the ship would not have sunk.

The big leak

By 12.00 a.m. Captain Smith knew that, as the weight of the water in the compartments pulled the bow of the ship downwards, the water would flow over the top of the compartments.

Morse code

Morse code is a set of dots, dashes, and spaces that can be sent, via an electric current, to the headset of an operator who translates the message. The process is instantaneous, which means Morse code messages can be received as they are being sent.

Morse code
a ●▬
b ▬●●●
c ▬●▬●
d ▬●●
e ●
f ●●▬●
g ▬▬●
h ●●●●
i ●●
j ●▬▬▬
k ▬●▬
l ●▬●●
m ▬▬
n ▬●
o ▬▬▬
p ●▬▬●
q ▬▬●▬
r ●▬●
s ●●●
t ▬
u ●●▬
v ●●●▬
w ●▬▬
x ▬●●▬
y ▬●▬▬
z ▬▬●●

TASK 1

Translate the following phrase into Morse code:

a) Struck iceberg, sinking fast

TASK 1

Use the Morse code to decipher the three following messages:

a) ▬●▬● ▬▬●▬ ▬●●
b) ●●● ▬▬▬ ●●●
c) ▬ ●▬ ●▬ ▬● ●●▬ ▬●▬●

View of the bridge

The *Titanic's* bridge contained telephones for contacting the rest of the ship, alarm bells, the control for closing the watertight doors, and telegraphs connected to the engine room. The ship's speed was controlled by officers on the bridge, who sent orders to the engine room via the telegraphs.

A telegraph

This telegraph, lying on the seabed, is from the docking bridge at the stern of the *Titanic*.

Marconi men

In 1912 all wireless communication was through Morse code. Just after midnight the *Titanic's* two wireless operators were both in the Marconi room when Captain Smith told them to put out a distress call.

The Marconi operators used Morse code to send their messages.

Danger signals

The letters "CQ" were the traditional distress signal. By adding a "D" the signal meant that assistance was needed. The Marconi room used this signal until one of the operators remembered the new signal "SOS". The *Titanic* was the first liner ever to transmit this signal.

"MGY" was the *Titanic's* call sign.

The bulkheads were supposed to contain any leaks, but the water flowed over the top of them.

The post office, directly above the mail room, started to flood at 11.55 p.m.

This message was picked up by a ship called the *Carpathia*, which was over 93 km (58 miles) away from the *Titanic*.

Watertight doors

The hull was divided by bulkheads into 16 compartments. Access between them was through the watertight doors. On the night of the disaster, although the doors were closed, the bulkheads were not high enough to prevent water from flowing over the top, from one compartment to the next.

Women and Children First

We are now just above the *Titanic*'s boat deck. All that remains are a few of the davits that were used to lower the lifeboats on the night of the disaster. This is one of the saddest places on the wreck – the sinking of the ship was one of the worst ever maritime disasters because there were not enough lifeboats for everyone to escape. Over two-thirds of the people on board the *Titanic* died on that terrible night.

Lifeboat davit
The British Board of Trade regulations required the *Titanic* to carry at least 16 lifeboats. Although the White Star Line exceeded these regulations by four, the *Titanic* could easily have carried far more lifeboats on the cleverly designed davits, which were capable of carrying more than one lifeboat each.

This davit was used to lower a lifeboat into the water.

Evacuation procedure
Soon after midnight, Captain Smith gave the order to prepare the lifeboats. He said that the women and children should evacuate the *Titanic* before the men. The first lifeboat touched the water at 12.25 a.m. on 15 April 1912. It carried less than half of its capacity of 65.

Captain Smith probably expected the half-empty lifeboats to come back to pick up people in the water. Unfortunately only one did.

AN OVERHEAD VIEW OF THE *TITANIC*'S DECKS

The lifeboats could hold a maximum of 65 people.

False safety
At first, few passengers believed that the *Titanic* was really sinking. On such a cold night, people were afraid of being lowered in an open boat 18 m (60 ft) down to the water below. During the evacuation, the crew had difficulty persuading people to get into the lifeboats.

Emergency plan
This plan shows the number of evacuation boats available. There were 14 lifeboats, two emergency boats, and four collapsible boats.

Going down
The *Titanic* finally sank at 2.20 a.m. on 15 April 1912. As her bow dipped underwater there were still many people huddled on her rising stern. Finally, the stern rose almost straight up and slid under the water.

THE RESCUE
The *Titanic*'s distress messages were picked up by many ships in the area. All steamed towards the *Titanic*, but none reached her before she sank. The *Carpathia* arrived first. At 4.10 a.m. her crew started to pick up the survivors and by 8 a.m. they were all safely on board.

The "life jacket"
There were enough life jackets for the passengers and crew, but they gave no protection against the freezing sea. Most people died of the cold, not by drowning.

TITANIC MYSTERY

As the *Titanic* was sinking, officers saw a ship about five or six miles away. They tried to signal with a Morse lamp, but the ship vanished. Who was she and why did she ignore the *Titanic*?

The collapsible boats could hold a maximum of 47 people.

The emergency boats could hold a maximum of 40 people.

Chance of survival
In 1912, ships were not required to carry lifeboats to hold all the passengers. After the *Titanic* disaster, the British Board of Trade regulations updated the lifeboat requirements of passenger ships.

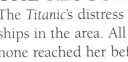

Boats on board the *Titanic*

14 lifeboats
2 emergency boats
4 collapsible boats

TASK 1
The lifeboats could hold 65 people each, the emergency boats 40 people each, and the collapsible boats 47 people each. Work out how many passengers and crew could have left the *Titanic* safely.

TASK 2
There were 2,206 passengers and crew on board the *Titanic*. What percentage of them had a chance of getting into a lifeboat?

TASK 3
1,503 people died when the *Titanic* sank. How many died because the lifeboats were not full?

Source for victims/survivors: the British Inquiry.

Bruce Ismay sent this message from the *Carpathia* to International Mercantile Marine, the owners of the White Star Line.

Unlucky escape
Bruce Ismay, White Star Line chairman, was a passenger on the *Titanic*. He helped load the lifeboats, but by getting into one himself he ruined his reputation, unlike Captain Smith, who went down with his ship.

Collapsible boat D
This was the last lifeboat to leave the *Titanic* and it reached the *Carpathia* at 7 a.m. Its passengers had spent nearly five hours waiting to be rescued.

Survivors on the *Carpathia*
The *Carpathia* had been on her way from New York to Gibraltar. Now she headed back to New York.

Touring the Seabed

"Hello. I'm Diana Barton, the conservator on board the *Nadir*. I'll be advising you, through *Nautile*'s underwater telephone, on how to recover objects from the seabed for an exhibition."

■ We are now approaching the debris field. When the *Titanic* sank, she broke in half and a great many objects, large and small, tumbled out and floated down to the bottom of the ocean. Over the years, some of the objects have disappeared, some have deteriorated, and some are still in perfect condition. The remaining debris now lies scattered over the seabed to the south of the stern.

THE DEBRIS FIELD

Most objects are lying on top of the seabed, but because there is a current, some of the small items may have been covered by silt. You will not see much life here. There are a few fish, crabs, and shrimps living off algae, but plants cannot exist because there is no light.

Rat-tailed fish can be seen swimming around the wreck.

Debris spotting
The only visual aids you have are the lights on the front of *Nautile*, so you need a mixture of careful observation and good luck to help you find objects.

Glazed objects
Many of the delicate glass and china objects are undamaged. These items came to rest gently on the silt on the seabed.

The "rusticles" break off if touched by *Nautile*.

Iron age
You will notice that the ship is covered with rust that looks like icicles. These are called "rusticles" and are formed by iron-eating bacteria. "Rusticles" grow until they fall off under their own weight.

The wooden crates have been eaten away, leaving the dishes perfectly stacked.

Wood borers
These ceramic dishes probably fell to the seabed in a wooden packing crate. All the soft wood was eaten away by wood-boring molluscs years ago.

Well dressed

Most clothing would have disintegrated during the first few years on the seabed. In some cases, however, shoes have survived. Leather is more resilient than cotton and wool.

Records of the past

Many of the objects give a uniquely detailed insight into the world of 1912. This letter was completely black when it was found on the seabed. It was restored in a laboratory and is now readable.

The letter comments on the fashion of wearing a feather boa.

Artefacts that have been immersed in seawater for years are porous and fragile and must be handled with care.

Bench mark

This frame from a deck bench is made of cast bronze and its years underwater have not caused any serious damage. However, it has absorbed chlorides and sulphides from the water, which have weakened and stained it.

HELPING HAND

The pressure of the water outside *Nautile* is so great it is impossible for you to leave the safety of the submersible. You must rely on *Nautile*'s articulated (jointed) arms, and their special tool attachments, to place objects from the debris field into the lifting baskets.

Nautile's pilot operates the arms from inside the submersible.

Heavy load

This heavy safe is virtually weightless underwater. *Nautile*'s arms use the clamp attachments to grip the awkward shape.

★ E X P L O R E R ' S   T A S K   J

Preservation of objects

At the bottom of the sea it is cold, there is no light, and the oxygen levels are low. These conditions slow down deterioration, but objects still suffer varying degrees of damage. Different materials deteriorate at different rates:

- Soft organic material, such as food, clothing, and wood, is at the greatest risk from fish and bacteria
- Marine worms bore holes in anything wooden
- Inorganic material, such as metal, ceramic, and glass, deteriorates more slowly, but it, too, is under threat
- Steel and iron are weakened by bacteria, but bronze objects are hardly affected
- Glass survives best of all

TASK 1

Using the information provided, list the following items in the order in which you would expect them to deteriorate. Start with the item that would deteriorate most quickly.

a) a champagne bottle   b) a loaf of bread
c) a solid bronze bench frame   d) a wooden shelf

Delicate touch

Nautile's arms have several attachments, a shovel, a sucker, and a gripper, for picking up delicate objects.

This plate is being picked up with the sucker attachment.

Nautile's arm can grip china without breaking it.

Returning to the *Nadir*

■ It is time to return to the surface. *Nautile* will drop her weights – the bags of steel shot – and you will start to rise gently through the water. An hour and a half later, you will notice the water get lighter and lighter, until finally you reach the surface. There, the objects you placed in the lifting baskets will have already been raised and taken on board the *Nadir*, ready for you to record and clean them.

SURFACING IN *NAUTILE*

The *Nadir* monitors *Nautile's* position as she rises. Just before *Nautile* breaks the surface, a diving team is sent out in an inflatable boat. Their job is to fasten ropes to *Nautile* so that she can be guided towards the *Nadir*.

The flag is used for spotting the basket on the surface.

The floats are made of tiny glass beads.

Transponder

This lifting basket contains dustbins for raising small items.

Old ships' chains are used as weights.

Lifting baskets

To raise the baskets from the seabed, a signal is sent to the transponder from the *Nadir*. This signal activates a mechanism on the basket that releases the chain weights so that the baskets slowly float up to the surface of the ocean.

Landing history

The lifting baskets are raised and pulled back on board the *Nadir* while *Nautile* is still on the seabed. This is to prevent any possible collisions or entanglements between them.

This is one of the open lifting baskets used to raise larger objects.

Back to mother

The most difficult part of the whole operation is when the *Nadir* lifts *Nautile* out of the water. You cannot leave *Nautile* until she is safely secured on the deck of the *Nadir*.

Emptying the baskets

The baskets are unloaded on the stern of the *Nadir* and the objects carried to the conservation laboratory on board. Smaller objects are wrapped in foam or bubble wrap and stored in trays for the voyage home.

The team will make special carrying frames for the larger objects, like this deck bench.

Hosing down

A large amount of mud is always brought up from the seabed with the basket. The mud is quite acidic and very smelly, but a high-pressure hose, which uses some of the *Nadir*'s valuable fresh water supply, is used to take off the worst of it.

Washing up

It is vital to keep objects immersed in water or they will start to deteriorate. It is also important to wash away the salts that have penetrated the objects.

Security check

On your return you will be asked for a list of all the objects you saw being picked up from the seabed. It will be checked with a list of everything that arrived on the *Nadir*. This way, there is no possibility of anything going missing.

All the items can be checked again with the video footage of the dive.

Surviving on the seabed

At sea level the pressure of the atmosphere around us is relatively constant. The deeper you go underwater, the higher the pressure level becomes. The pressure pushes in on flexible air spaces, compressing them and reducing their volume. The air is not lost, it is simply compressed.

TASK 1

A number of champagne bottles sank with the *Titanic*. As they fell, air inside the bottles, in between the champagne and the cork, was compressed by the pressure of the water outside. When the wreck was found 76 years later, what do you think the champagne bottles looked like when they were raised?

a) the corks had been pushed inside the bottles
b) the bottles had exploded
c) the corks had been pushed out of the bottles
d) the corks were intact

PRESERVING THE PAST

Before the objects can be displayed in an exhibition they must be cleaned up. Much of this work uses dangerous chemicals, which could easily spill on a ship at sea. So the full conservation treatment will take place in a laboratory on dry land.

Salty cherub

The green streaks on this bronze cherub are a product of corrosion. The cherub must be treated to make its condition stable or it will deteriorate rapidly.

Surface salts are simply washed out using fresh water.

Electrolysis treatment

Removing the salts trapped inside the cherub is difficult. It is done by connecting the cherub to a power supply and placing it in a chemical bath lined with a stainless steel grid. The salts are attracted to the current, so as the current passes from the cherub to the grid, it takes the salts along with it.

Salt water reacts with bronze to create a corrosive green coating called verdigris.

Index

Picture credits

Every effort has been made to trace the copyright holders. Dorling Kindersley apologizes for any unintentional omissions and would be pleased, in such cases, to add an acknowledgment in future editions. The publisher would like to thank the following individuals, companies, and picture libraries for their kind permission to reproduce their photographs: Mary Evans Picture Library: 19cr, 23crb, c, 29br; The Hulton Getty Picture Collection Ltd: 22cl, cr; Ifremer: 11cla, c, 31c; Illustrated London News: 19cl; The Irish Picture Library: 21cr, br, tl F.R. Browne Collection; MacQuitty International Collection: 12c, 14tr, 23cl, 25tr; Ken Marschall Collection: 15bc, 17c, 19clb; National Geographic: 6tr, 8br, 12tr, 13tc, 14bc, 16tr, 17tc, 18cl Emory Kristof; National Maritime Museum: 12bl, 13bc; Rex Features: 6cr, 14bc, br, 15tl, bc, br, 16cr, 18tr, bl, 21cb, 23tl, cr, 24br, 27bc, ca, bc, 28cl, tr, cr, bl, cb, 29ca, bc/11tc Nils Jorgansen/9tc R. Sobol; Frank Spooner Pictures: 4br, 9bl, 14bl, 18cr, 21c, 24clb, 26cra, 27cr, 29cl; Sygma: 9cl, 10tr, cr, 15bl, 20tr, 24cra, c, 25tc, cla, bl, cb, br, 26br, 27tl, ca, bl, 28br, 29tl, tc, cl; Ulster Folk & Transport Museum: 9tr, 13cl, 17c; Woods Hole Oceanographic Institute: 9tl. Jacket: Ken Marschall Collection: front cla; Ulster Folk & Transport Museum: front ca; National Maritime Museum: front bc; Sygma: front clb.

☆⚑ EXPLORER'S TASK ANSWERS

Explorer's Task A
Task 1 – The Azores
Task 2 – New York (76° W, 40° N)
Task 3 – No, the ship has sailed past the Equator (0°) and the North Star has dropped below the horizon.

Explorer's Task B
Task 1 – b
Task 2 – Nø, since the seabed is uneven the echoes would come back at different times depending on how deep each part of it was.

Explorer's Task C
Task 1
a – 1,000 m (3,280 ft)
b – 1,500 m (4,920 ft)
c – 2,000 m (6,560 ft)

Explorer's Task D
Task 1
a – sink, b – float, c – float

Explorer's Task E
Task 1 – 2,435 passengers

Explorer's Task F
Task 1 – 6,000 tonnes (5,905 tons)

Explorer's Task G
Task 1 – 100,000 m³ (3,531,000 ft³)
Task 2 – 112,500 m³ (3,972,375 ft³)

Explorer's Task H
Task 1
••• – •–• ••– –•– –•–
–• –•–• • ––• ––•• – – –
••• •• –• –•– •– ••– – –
••–• •– ••• –
Task 2
a) – CQD, b) – SOS, c) – *Titanic*

Explorer's Task I
Task 1 – 1,178 passengers and crew
Task 2 – 53.5%
Task 3 – 475 people

Explorer's Task J
Task 1 – b), d), c), a)

Explorer's Task K
Task 1 – a) and occasionally d) when the liquid in the bottle fills right up to the cork, leaving no air to be compressed.

The expedition leaders featured in this book are fictitious and any resemblance to actual persons, living or dead, is purely coincidental.

Acknowledgments

Dorling Kindersley would like to thank the following people for their contributions to this book: Stephen Bull for the explorer's task illustrations, Paul Bampton and Eryl Davies for consultancy on the explorer's tasks, and Ryan Davis.